The Great Houses of New Orleans

The Great Houses of New Orleans

....

WRITTEN AND PHOTOGRAPHED

BY *Curt Bruce*

ARCH CAPE PRESS

NEW YORK

This 1986 edition is published by Arch Cape Press,
distributed by Crown Publishers, Inc., by arrangement with
Alfred A. Knopf, Inc.

FRONTISPIECE: GALLIER HOUSE WINDOW,
1118-32 ROYAL STREET

The photographs and illustrations on pages 26, 27, 29, 33, 48,
and 49 are reproduced with permission from the collection of the
Louisiana State Museum. The maps on pages 9 and 10 are
reproduced with permission from the collection of the New Orleans
Public Library. The drawings on page 46 are reproduced with the
permission of the Historic New Orleans Collection.

Printed and Bound in the United States of America

Library of Congress Cataloging in Publication Data
Bruce, Curt.
The great houses of New Orleans.
Reprint. Originally published: 1st ed. New York :
Knopf, 1977.
Includes index.
1. Dwellings—Louisiana—New Orleans.
2. Architecture, Domestic—Louisiana—New Orleans.
3. New Orleans (La.)—Buildings, structures, etc.
I. Title.
NA7238.N5B78   1986   728'.09763'35   86-3619
ISBN *0-517-61523-1*

Book design by Camilla Filancia

h g f e d c b a

To GINGER *and* ARKY

ROBBINS

Contents

. . . .

Author's Note

I was fortunate to be able to shoot the photographs for *The Great Houses of New Orleans* during the late spring and early summer of 1975. Fortunate in the sense that the skies of this season are in a state of constant metamorphosis, swept by cumulus, stratus, nimbostratus, and of course the thick, dark thunderheads that sweep in off the Delta to drench the bend in the river with abundant precipitation. Getting rained out is one disadvantage of working in New Orleans at this time of year. Many times I had to escape with my equipment into the sumptuous confines of a saloon to wait out a downpour. Usually, the fierce Southern sun would break out again, revealing some of the most extraordinary and breathtaking skies I'd ever seen—rivaling those of Holland and the South Pacific—fitting backdrops for the exquisite architecture of the Crescent City.

It was always best to start shooting as early as possible, for the temperature and the humidity would climb proportionately as the morning progressed. Shooting became a contest against the sun, or "How long can one stay on the street?"—a break for lunch and then back out again. Of course, if I was shooting Uptown or in the Garden District, the shade was some compensation, but it's not unusual for the street temperatures to hit a hundred in the shade by the afternoon. Many times, it was only the excellent root beer sold at all the little neighborhood groceries that enabled me to keep at it.

I tried every approach possible in shooting the book, but most of the reconnaissance work wound up being done on foot, as usually happens. It takes the slow pace of the pedestrian to brake the eye, allowing one to perceive almost every detail of a block or street. I had hoped to use my ten-speed bicycle in New Orleans, since the flatness of the city makes it ideal for cycling. But this technique proved to be better for getting around to locations than for finding them, and the temperatures always intervened, preventing too much pedaling for very long. I was able to use my van to good advantage. It is equipped with a skylight of ¾-inch Plexiglas that covers the entire front of the roof, allowing visibility that is usually possible only in a convertible. It was quite useful for stopping and contemplating a façade while pondering whether or not to shoot it, or for cruising slowly while keeping an eye peeled above for that special gable or porch detail.

Technically, the photography was done with the use of two Hasselblad cameras, a 500 C and a Super-Wide C. The film was Kodak Plus-X. I use a Tiltall tripod, and the negatives were printed on Agfa Brovira paper.

It might be wise to include a note on the designation "Creole" as it is used in New Orleans, since there is great confusion as to exactly who the Creoles are. They are often thought to be Cajuns, the French Canadian immigrants to the bayous, or the varied black populace of the city (who did create most of the outstanding "Creole" recipes which are so deservedly famous). In cooking, "Creole" means simply "with tomatoes or tomato sauce"; in anthropology, "an isolated pocket of settlers preserving the customs and traditions of their mother site." In New Orleans, it's a somewhat bastardized idea, but "Creole" refers to the French and Spanish settlers and their descendants simultaneously, and was used to distinguish them from the Americans.

I want to say here that I've never worked in any other place that combines the relaxed, live-and-let-live atmosphere of New Orleans, for which it is duly famous, with the generosity and helpfulness of the populace. In doing any sort of historical documentary work, it is necessary to secure the aid of historical societies, museums, picture archives, and historians while shaping the overall form of one's concept. Help from many different parties is a necessity, and in New Orleans it is offered with a casual and interested air that really is impressive.

I want to thank the following individuals and institutions for their assistance while I was working on location in New Orleans—they help to make New Orleans the great place that it remains today: Mr. Samuel L. Wilson, Jr., who has done so much to raise the level of appreciation of New Orleans architecture through his restorative architectural work and historical writings; Mr. Richard Krotzler, Jr., the architect who pointed me in the direction of many rare masterpieces of local design; Ms. Nadine Russel, Director of Gallier House, and her entire staff, who made working in that impressive building a rewarding experience; Mr. Stanton Frazer, Director of the fascinating Historic New Orleans Collection, and his staff, who kindly opened the archives under their care to my scrutiny; Mr. J. B. Harter, Curator of the Louisiana State Museum, who was generous with both his time and his collection while I worked in those archives. Dick Allen, Curator of the William Ransom Hogan Collection at Tulane (the "Jazz Museum"),

. . . .

was also extremely helpful. At the New Orleans Public Library, Ernest "Tito" Braun, of the Louisiana Division, was a great help while I was working there.

Among the citizens of New Orleans I was grateful for the generosity of Mrs. Clare W. Beales, Mrs. Audrey Brooks, Mr. Gordon Ewin, Mr. and Mrs. Richard Freeman, Jr., the Garden District Association, Mr. and Mrs. Leland S. Montgomery, Mr. and Mrs. James D. Mullins, Mr. Ray Samuels, and Mr. and Mrs. Roger P. Sharp. My friends and associates who have made invaluable contributions to the book are: Marjorie Aronson, Roger and Betty Baird, Jim Ballintyne, Curtis B. Bruce II, Cliff Coulston, Lionel Craven, Crescenzo Giasullo, Mr. and Mrs. Ed Hauben, the redoubtable George Hoffberg, Dean Kirkpatrick, Beverly Labin, Linda Lieberman, Philip Makanna, Barry Silberstang, Monica Suder, Marjorie Trites, and Jim and Ellen Tyack.

For work on the book itself, I want to extend a special acknowledgment to two people who contributed greatly to its creation: my editor, Ann Close, whose encouragement and trust have been inspirational; and Mary Letterii, whose tireless research resulted in the text and who helped in more ways than I can say.

WALL OF ST. LOUIS CEMETERY, BASILICA OF ST. LOUIS, CHARTRES STREET, JACKSON SQUARE

. . . .

Tales of the Great City

. . . .

When Jack Kerouac's Sal Paradise left the urban college in search of experience that would ignite and give credence to his dream of the real America, he was equipped with but the barest essentials and an unfaltering faith in his own intuition. He was to taste the essence of the land in transitory encounters along the side of some desolate Interstate, in the vineyards of California, in the steamy darkness of a Fifty-seventh Street jazz dive, yet all this "road" had been paved for him by the wandering, restless spirit of his fellow countrymen.

Americans have always reached over the edge and broken their boundaries, and have always sought the dimension attained only through the most intense experience. The special state of consciousness reached by way of shattering all one's previous conditioning is truly the realm of the unknown. The longing for this mystery was present long before there was a flag, a Constitution, or the concept of a country. Searching, driven, working, and fighting, the countless pioneers, seamen, scouts, traders, and land rovers of all varieties cut their imprint into the native landscape.

Separated by the time span of three quarters of a century, Mark Twain's Huck Finn and Kerouac's Paradise were united in their quest for the livable American city, a Gotham where their pained sense of the real would be subdued beneath the warm glow of a Utopian ideal. Travelers and adventurers (but travelers foremost), Finn and Paradise both found shelter in New Orleans, and their creators wrote about the city with admiration.

Suffering from acute wanderlust and restlessness during their earlier years, Twain and Kerouac both moved farther and farther away from the social nexus of their respective eras. And the outsiders like them, the strangers, the bohemians, have left their mark on the city of New Orleans from the time when the first meager foundations were sunk into the black loam of the Mississippi River Delta. A creation of wanderers, misfits, and pirates of every persuasion, the city has a locale as improbable as its history, a swamp on the great brown aorta, the Mississippi River.

. . . .

To the outsider, especially anyone swimming beyond the mainstream of American life, New Orleans, because it *is* so foreign, because other flags flew above it long before the American, has proved to be a place where would-be expatriates would find succor and a place they could call "home." During the first part of the century, while Stein and Hemingway were holding court in Paris, New Orleans was beginning to enjoy residents such as the writer Sherwood Anderson. Attracted to the French Quarter by its thick aroma of the exotic, he bought a small cottage in the then dilapidated neighborhood. Only the possessor of a sensitive eye would be inspired to move there by choice, a person tuned to the textures of the crumbling masonry, the tired balconies, and the abundant craftsmanship that makes those streets a living museum.

It is easy, ambling along a cobbled block in the oldest part of town—the Vieux Carré—to be conscious of the weight of time and the taste of the past. Where else can you feel like a foreigner in your own country? The openness and graciousness of New Orleans is immediately felt by the most casual visitor. Where else is there an American city that has fostered such a full, rich mythology that continues to grow today? Where else is there an American city whose living heritage is part of a historical greatness that attracted the attention of several civilizations and even the entire world? New Orleans' past isn't just institutionalized in its museums and historical societies, or between the covers of countless books about it, but is alive in the streets and walkways, in the walls and parapets, the slate roofs and chimney pots of Jackson Square, and in every antique building.

The people of the city are proud of their past. They know its history. They can talk for hours about it; more can be learned from such a conversation than from a week's research. And they really have something to be proud of. Their environment is testament to the richness and creativity of their past. The sense of custom and tradition that is so sadly lacking in the monotonous sea of contemporary America is a way of life in New Orleans. The French and Spanish tongues, the cuisines, the oral history, the Krewes and the costumes of Mardi Gras, the jazz—all leave an impression that is rich and unique in the mediocre, dreary landscape of the later twentieth century.

So drift down the Mississippi to that peculiar, foreign, and most mysterious of all American cities. Perhaps sometime in the late-night stillness, the reflection of the past ages the city has known may reappear and breathe as the curtain of time slowly rises on the legends and legendary, the quixotic twists of fate that shaped the eras of New Orleans' greatness. The walls have gazed on the abundant life that has thronged through these blocks, and the story behind these buildings, the creations and their creators, is the one we're going to tell now.

The sea birds soared and hung in the air on the day René Robert Cavalier, Sieur de La Salle, and his expedition sailed down the Mississippi into the bayou-laden Delta, claiming the river and all the land through which they had passed for King and France. Since he had descended the Mississippi from its source near the Canadian border, La Salle's claim proved to be the most extensive one ever made by a European power on the North American continent. It also marked the beginning of France's long preoccupation with its newly named Louisiana Territory.

In the year 1684, two years following that momentous voyage, Louis XIV, the Sun King, commanded that a permanent settlement be established in the unknown region which had so recently been added to his overseas empire. He again sent La Salle, this time to found a colony at a strategic location near the mouth of the Mississippi. But the expedition ended in disaster. A faulty navigational calculation left the party shipwrecked in eastern Texas, far west of its destination; and disease and attacks of local Indian tribes led to a mutiny, during which La Salle was assassinated by one of his own men.

News of the great explorer's untimely death put a damper on French plans to colonize Louisiana, and for the next fourteen years Louis neglected his ambitions for the New World. It was not until a rumor reached the Court of Versailles that England planned to settle the region that the King felt compelled to send two brothers, Pierre and Jean le Moyne, Sieurs d'Iberville and de Bienville, to relocate the entry to his Louisiana Territory. In that same year, 1698, a small flotilla of four vessels set sail from Brest intent on establishing a French foothold in the bayous of Louisiana.

The King's selection of leaders was excellent, for it was the resourcefulness and determination of Iberville and Bienville that made the venture possible. It is difficult today to grasp the problems of starting a livable community where nothing exists. At the turn of the eighteenth century, the myriad hardships facing settlers in Louisiana's wilderness were almost insurmountable. The area was lacking in every amenity of civilization, and the unfamiliar semitropical climate wreaked havoc with the colonists' best-laid plans. The colonies in the islands of the West Indies and the Spanish settlements of Mexico couldn't be counted on to provide aid for France's colonial effort, and the length of the sea voyage made communication with the mother country feeble and tenuous. Yet despite these adversities, the French managed to establish three small but hardy villages at the present sites of Natchez,

. . . .

Biloxi, and Mobile. And by 1712, after years of arduous deprivation, three hundred souls peopled these towns; life in the young colony was fragile yet enduring.

Back in France, existence in the colony was viewed from a totally unrealistic perspective. Many an idle dandy, strolling the boulevards of Paris in his lacy finery, inhaling a pinch of lavender snuff, accepted the then popular myths that Louisiana abounded with pearl fisheries, gold and silver mines, and beneficent savages quite eager to grant any request of their European guests. These notions were entertained by most French subjects and were soon to be exploited by Monsieur John Law and his notorious Company of the West.*

One of the more remarkable characters to play a major role in the development of Louisiana, John Law was both a scoundrel and a complex and authentic genius. The son of an aristocratic Scottish family, Law had squandered a fortune by the age of twenty, then had regained and improved upon the original at Europe's gaming tables. His talents and ready wealth provided easy access to the French court, and in short order he maneuvered to have himself appointed financial minister to Philip, Duke of Orléans, regent of France.

Listening to the tales of a wealthy Parisian banker just returned from trying to develop the supposedly vast mineral resources of Louisiana, Law soon saw a way in which to take full advantage of his new and powerful position. He suggested to Philip that Louisiana could best be exploited by a powerful government holding company, in which public shares would be sold. Any plan to help ease the ponderous national debt appealed to the regent, and in September of 1717 the Company of the West came into being, with Monsieur Law appointed supreme director. This institution dominated and controlled the destiny of Louisiana for the next twenty-five years.

Troubles between the Company, with its wildly misdirected plans for the colony, and the settlers, whose concerns were more down to earth, started while the first shares were being gobbled up by eager Parisians. Bienville had long dreamed of establishing a port town near the entrance of the Mississippi to control the potentially enormous volume of trade that he foresaw the river would one day carry. After careful exploration, he had even selected a spot, a place the Indians used for portage between the Mississippi and Lake Pontchartrain, some thirty leagues from the Gulf of Mexico. It had the excellent natural advantage of being high enough above the river to be fairly solid, and the surrounding land was rich and fertile. The Com-

---

* Albert Phelps, *Louisiana* (New York, 1905), pp. 60–1.

. . . .

6

pany, focused only on mining precious metals and quick wealth, had not the slightest interest in such a project and refused support. When Iberville died, Bienville was appointed governor in his place. With his position secure, he acted rapidly to fulfill his dream. In February of 1718 (though the exact date is uncertain), he landed with a group of workers at a bend in the river near an Indian village named Tchoutchouma and set to work clearing land for a settlement, which he named Nouvelle Orléans, in honor of the Duke.

In France, John Law's bogus publicity and fantastic stories, which continued to paint Louisiana as an earthly paradise, had by this time dangerously inflated the Company of the West stock. Law also used the tales as a means to procure recruits for the Company's "enterprises" in Louisiana. Etchings of this period depict cartloads of rabble leaving the walls of Paris en route to ships waiting to transport them to the mouth of the Mississippi. Every sort of criminal, the ill and the infirm, beggars, pimps, and whores, joined by naïve Frenchmen with golden ambitions, set out to reap the rewards that the wondrous colony offered. In one manner or another, John Law sent six thousand white settlers and three thousand black slaves to Bienville to aid in operating the Company's totally fictional gold and silver mines.*

Among the women John Law shipped to Louisiana in response to Bienville's complaint that his men, desperate for female company, were running in the woods after Indian maidens were former inmates of the notorious Parisian women's house of detention, La Salpêtrière. These unfortunates became known to the colonists as "the correction girls," and Law thoughtfully sent a midwife to accompany them. Although the correction girls were integrated into colonial society, not one of them produced any offspring, and the midwife remained unemployed.

Another boatload of women soon arrived, this time the daughters of poor but upright families. They were quickly dubbed "the casket girls," because John Law, in an uncharacteristically magnanimous gesture, had thought to provide each recruit with a small hope chest of clothes when she volunteered for the voyage. The casket girls continued to arrive periodically in New Orleans up until 1761 and, unlike their predecessors, proved to be very fertile.†

The complete lack of any mineral resources in the bayous eventually led to the Company of the West being nicknamed "the Mississippi Bubble Company," and when the bubble burst in 1720, as it was bound to do, the kingdom of France itself was brought to the edge of economic collapse. Monsieur Law prudently fled the country. Bienville was left with the problem of in-

---

* Herbert Asbury, *The French Quarter* (New York: Knopf, 1936), p. 2.
† Ibid., p. 81.

corporating large numbers of ill-prepared new arrivals into a colony that was already hard-pressed to feed and care for itself, and with twenty more years of dominance by the now much-chastened Company of the West.

The first buildings in New Orleans were erected by six carpenters, four Canadians, and thirty convicted salt thieves who had opted for a fresh start in Louisiana rather than serve out their jail terms. Adrien de Pauger, Second Engineer for France in Louisiana, was responsible for laying out the streets of the town as the colonists cleared the thick forest that grew down to the Mississippi's edge. He conceived a simple, gridlike pattern, a methodical interpretation of the classic Renaissance town plan. The original grid stretched for nine squares along the river and was six squares deep. Fronting on the river was a central square with buildings on three sides named the Place d'Armes; it became the heart of New Orleans.

The earliest houses were crude and basic structures, little more than temporary shelter until permanent accommodations could be constructed. Hastily thrown together from split timbers or logs with a mixture of moss and mud filling the chinks, they usually consisted of a single room. Nondescript barracks were erected for the soldiers and larger shelters were put up to house the officers and important members of the community. Within a few years, however, more substantial structures began to appear among the rough cabins. Often the plans for these houses and public buildings were drawn by royal architects and engineers, such as Blond de la Tour, Chief Engineer for France in Louisiana. The drawings were executed in the best traditions of Louis XV draftsmanship, providing builders with plan, elevation, and section. The first parish church, which stood on the spot where the Basilica of St. Louis stands today, was designed in this way by de la Tour.

The establishment of a brickyard on the outskirts of town, making stable foundations possible, greatly changed the nature of New Orleans' architecture. The water table under the town was so high that a hole dug in the earth to the depth of a foot would rapidly fill with water. Before brick foundations, the floors of the houses had been laid directly on the ground (*colombage sur sole*), causing them to rot from constant exposure to moisture. Trenches had to be dug around every block of the town to drain the ever-present fluid, and even so, the squares of the infant city remained marshy for many years. The advent of brick enabled the colonists to build more durable structures and opened up the possibilities for a greater variety of design.

The area surveyed by de Pauger was the nucleus of what would become the Vieux Carré. The squares were each 320 feet on a side; these in turn were divided into 60-foot lots. The original streets were laid out to be 38 feet 6 inches wide, and as the town grew through the eighteenth century this measurement was maintained to encompass nearly a hundred squares. The streets remain approximately this width today and have kept the names originally bestowed on them. From the outset, buildings were placed on the street line, which accentuated the urban character of the young city. The land surrounding the town's borders was parceled out in grants to planters, who developed it with slave labor. As New Orleans grew, so did the number of plantations adjoining and close to the city.

Early maps of New Orleans show designs for rather elaborate fortifica-

PROPOSED PLAN FOR NEW ORLEANS,
SHOWING FORTIFICATIONS NEVER ERECTED, CIRCA 1710

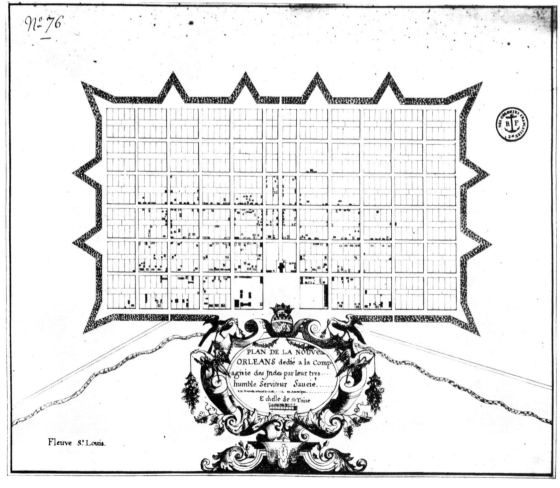

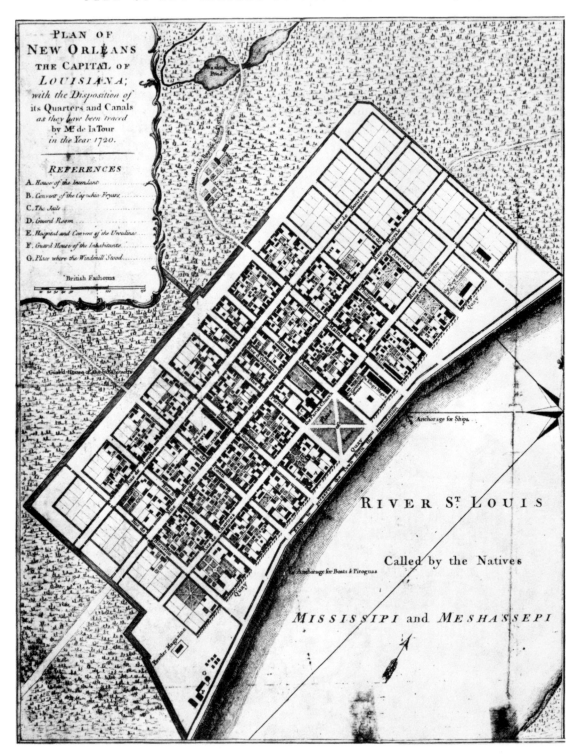

tions such as walls and moats, but since relations with the neighboring Indian tribes were excellent at first, these plans were not realized immediately. The major engineering contribution was the construction of earthen levees. They were built to a height of fifteen feet on the edge of the riverbank to keep back the high waters during floodtime. The river played havoc with the town in the first years of its existence, and the streets were annually turned into streams while the houses became small islets in the soupy muck. To a degree, the levee prevented this, but it often proved insufficient to withstand the river. The levee demanded constant maintenance and attention, and it had to be strengthened repeatedly throughout the colonial period.

As the design of the dwellings in New Orleans grew more sophisticated, the method of building known as split-timber construction (also widespread in Europe at the time) became popular. The builders would leave diagonal and horizontal beams exposed, filling the spaces between them with brick, which was then covered with mortar. Masonry buildings could only be of a single story, since a second story made them too heavy for the soggy ground. Split-timber construction was badly affected by the damp climate and was abandoned after a time when the buildings quickly started to decay and collapse. The first Ursuline Convent was built by this method and began to crumble before the second, larger convent building could be completed.

The Ursuline nuns had come to New Orleans in 1727 at Bienville's personal request. He had felt the colony was sorely lacking in attendant medical facilities and the means of educating the growing numbers of children. For the next hundred years, the Ursulines directed their efforts toward nursing and teaching, making unselfish and rich contributions to the life of the city. The second Ursuline Convent, located on Chartres Street, is one of the two examples of early New Orleans architecture that remain.

The other is a quaint colonial house of the period known fondly as Madame John's Legacy (12).* Madame John's is an early attempt at a two-story building. This famous residence (rebuilt in 1788) stands at 623 Dumaine Street. The original was built in 1726 by Jean Pascal, a sea captain from Provence, on a site granted him by the Company of the Indies. He lived there with his wife and daughter until he was killed in the Natchez massacre in 1729. In the seventeen-seventies, it was the home of René Beluche, the smuggler captain of the ship *Spy*. The house was named by the writer George W. Cable; in Cable's story, when a later owner of the

---

* The italicized numbers in parentheses, here and throughout this essay, refer to the pages on which a building or particular architectural style under discussion is pictured.

house, another Jean, was dying, he left the building to his quadroon mistress, Zalli, and their daughter 'Tite Poulette. The unfortunate Zalli sold the house and then lost all her profit when her bank failed.

Many of the houses and buildings of the French colonial period were characterized by a shingled roof with a low, sloping pitch, curved at the eaves. As time went on, the shingles were replaced with tile manufactured in the colony. The eaves later were extended, a feature that continued into the early nineteenth century. The shape was popular owing to the function it provided: protection from the heat of the sun and the ever-present moisture and rainstorms. The style was not confined to New Orleans, and traces of it can be seen frequently in older plantation design and in colonial architecture throughout the West Indies, from which it was derived. Madame John's and the West Indian Pitot House (*13*) on Bayou St. John both show strong elements of this genre.

Madame John's is an excellent example of the evolution of building

MADAME JOHN'S LEGACY, BOURBON AND DUMAINE STREETS, 1788

. . . .

techniques in the colony. The ground floor rises on brick piers, which support the second, lighter wooden floor and gallery under wide eaves and a broad roof. The ground floor could be used for business, cooking, and storage. The upper floor contained the living quarters of the occupants; galleries and shuttered windows provided a cool relief from the subtropical climate while catching any breeze which might blow that way. The popularity of this practical design was widespread.

Bienville was recalled to France, leaving the new city in the hands of the second governor, Etienne de Périer, who was not as sensitive to the delicate relationships between the colony and its Indian neighbors as his predecessor had been. Trouble began when the Natchez Indians learned that the French settlers near Fort Rosalie (now Natchez) were planning to usurp their lands. In retaliation, the tribe rallied and attacked the garrison. By an elaborate

PITOT HOUSE, BAYOU ST. JOHN, BUILT 1799

. . . .

13

ruse, the Indians caught the settlers unprepared, and in the ensuing slaughter 144 men, 35 women, and 56 children were slain.*

When news of the massacre and the continued breakdown in French-Indian relations reached Paris, Périer was recalled, and Bienville, now old, was reinstated as governor. But he made the error of attempting to regain face for the French by punishing the Natchez. He led two well-organized attacks against the Indians during the next seven years. Both failed, and Bienville finally handed in his resignation as governor. He returned to France and never set foot on Louisiana soil again.

The next governor, the Marquis Pierre de Vaudreuil, brought with him a lavish European style of living heretofore unseen anywhere in the New World. He was the personification of a French aristocrat and insisted on the best of everything—the latest fashions, and the refinements and trappings that he was accustomed to in Paris. The imported elegance at first mystified the common citizens still living in a city of unlit and muddy streets lined with clapboard houses, with snakes and reptiles slithering around in the marshy parts of town. But soon these manners and customs, unrestrained by any sense of Puritan morality on the part of the populace, took root and flourished and became part of the New Orleans way of life.

"The Grand Marquis," as he came to be known, went to great lengths to turn his remote outpost into a facsimile of the best Paris had to offer. He was responsible for introducing those elements which became the backbone of culture in New Orleans society: balls, banquets, the theater, and, eventually, opera. Early in his administration, he had the first play to be produced in the city performed in his mansion. It was called *The Indian Father*, and the Marquis himself figured in it.

Although de Vaudreuil's administration restored and maintained amicable and peaceful relations with the colony's Indian neighbors, the Marquis was the initiator of an unsavory tradition for which he is best remembered: he was the first in a dynasty of corrupt and shallow politicians who made the most out of their time in office. The Marquis practiced nepotism, handing out government positions readily to his and his wife's families, and he also found many creative ways to turn a profit. He frequently waylaid vital stores sent from France for the maintenance of New Orleans' troops and garrison. He would then market these quality goods (their value in Louisiana at that time was incalculable), while substituting provisions of an inferior quality in their place. Trade permits could be had by anyone willing to grease the Marquis' palm with a surreptitious bribe and a promise to cut him in on a share of the forthcoming profits.

* Lyle Saxon, *Fabulous New Orleans* (New Orleans: Crager & Co., 1928), pp. 113–114.

. . . .

The Intendant Commissary, Michel de la Rouvillière, described conditions in New Orleans under the Marquis in a letter addressed to the home office in Paris dated June 20, 1751:

> No justice is to be expected from Monsieur de Vaudreuil; he is too lazy, too negligent, his wife too malicious, too passionate, and has too strong interests in all the settlements, and in the town of New Orleans, not to prevail on him to keep on fair and even terms with others. . . . There is no discipline; the most indulgent toleration is granted to the soldiers, provided they drink their money at the licensed liquor shop where they are given drugs which ruin their health. . . . For several months, there has never been less than a hundred of them at the hospital. . . . The soldiers are allowed to do as they please, provided they drink at the liquor shop designated for them; and they carry out of it wine and spirits which they sell to the negroes and to the indians. . . .*

The influx of unsavory persons into Louisiana became almost as great as it had been during the height of the Mississippi Company's debacle. Drawn magnetically by the Marquis' lax rule, they helped add to the already degenerate state of affairs. In 1750, counterfeit currency was found in circulation throughout New Orleans. After much breast-beating, the Marquis managed to recapture one of the culprits, a free Negro named Joseph. Not only was most of de Vaudreuil's own fortune made worthless by this turn of events, but, to his further embarrassment, he discovered that his government had issued the bogus bills! He ordered that Joseph be flogged publicly, be branded on the shoulder with the fleur-de-lys, and be sold into slavery in Santo Domingo.† Having taken care of the counterfeiter, the Marquis drew up some thirty new articles of law for New Orleans, in an effort to restrain the epidemic of criminal activity that had devastated even his personal bank account. This was his final act in office, for he was soon appointed governor of Canada.

He was replaced by a former captain of the French navy, Louis Billouart, Chevalier de Kerlerec, who became the fourth governor of the city. He arrived in New Orleans in February of 1753 and, true to the manner of the departed regime, threw a showy state dinner both for the outgoing Marquis and to celebrate his own ascent to the command post. Two fountains of wine flowed for the common folk of New Orleans, and in the evening they were treated to an extravagant fireworks display. Although this celebration seemed to indicate that business would continue as usual, New Orleans was actually on the verge of even grimmer and more austere times.

---

* Asbury, *The French Quarter*, p. 25.
† Ibid.

· · · · · · · · · · ·

Kerlerec's administration was concurrent with the complex and futile Seven Years' War in Europe, during which England and France struggled for possession of Canada; although New Orleans was physically removed from the action, it was subject to the war's shock waves. As the conflict dragged on, the city's vital lifeline to Europe was severed by pirates and privateers plying the Atlantic and Gulf Coast who frequently intercepted most of the supplies bound for New Orleans.

The Seven Years' War ended officially in 1763, with the ratification of the Treaty of Paris. France ceded all of her American territory east of the Mississippi to England in this agreement, with the added clause that English merchant vessels would be free to travel the Mississippi without a tariff. At the same time, Spain ceded Florida to England and gained Cuba, which had been in English hands. It was widely assumed that France would retain control of Louisiana, but by way of a secret arrangement made in late 1762, Louisiana and New Orleans became the dominion of the King of Spain.

Two years elapsed before the residents of Louisiana even received word of what had happened, and it was seven years before the Spanish exercised control. The French colonists had felt bitterly betrayed by their fatherland and had sent a representative to petition Louis XV to retain the city. When Louis refused even to see them, they began to talk about armed resistance to Spain and the formation of a free republic in the Territory. This was enough to frighten off the first governor sent by Spain, an action that in the end had dire consequences for the conspirators.

On August 18, 1769, Don Alexander O'Reilly, an Irish count who had become a great European general in the service of Spain, sailed up the river to New Orleans with twenty-four warships, fifty pieces of artillery, and a hand-picked army of over three thousand men. In a formal ceremony at the Place d'Armes, he raised the flag of Spain over the city, and with this impressive show of might, immediately dispelled any further thoughts of rebellion.

O'Reilly then publicly executed the ringleaders of the French opposition, whom he had tricked into surrendering, an act and a display for which the Creoles never forgave him. After almost a half-century of suffering and sweating to defeat the heavy odds against them, the French of New Orleans found themselves powerless beneath the forceful and hated rule of Spain and its occupying army. In resigned and oppressive silence, the whole city watched while the street names were changed from French to Spanish, and Spanish became the official language of the colony. Even the Ursuline Sisters were ordered to recite their prayers from Spanish prayer books.

. . . .

The census ordered by O'Reilly at the time he took the city shows a population of 3,190 persons of all ages, sexes, and colors, with 1,225 of these being slaves, along with 60 captured Indians. (The Spanish forbade the holding of Indians as slaves.)

O'Reilly maintained a severe and intense domination over New Orleans for the next year and a half before passing the reins of power over to a milder succession of Spanish governors general. Relations between the Creoles and the Spanish who moved into the city as the regime became entrenched eventually began to reach a level of equanimity. The changes wrought by Spain remained, but the heart of the city remained Creole, and the French also continued to greatly outnumber the Spanish.

After surviving floods, hurricanes, reptiles, the armada of O'Reilly, and the threat of Indian massacre, New Orleans succumbed to the devastation of an enormous fire, which swept through the city on Good Friday of 1788. The smoke was first seen on Chartres Street as it poured out of the home of Don Vincento José Núñez, the Military Treasurer of the colony. A taper had fallen against the lace drapes of the altar in the Don's home and the building was soon on fire. Within minutes there was no stopping the inferno, which raced through the ramshackle wooden buildings, spreading easily from one to another. The *Gazette de Deux Ponts* of August, 1788, carried the following description:

> All the vigilance of the official chiefs and the prompt assistance which they brought to bear, were useless and even the engines, many of which were burned by the heat of the flames at an incredible distance. In order to appreciate the horror of the conflagration, it suffices to say that in less than five hours eight hundred and sixteen buildings were reduced to ashes, comprising in the number all commercial houses except three, and the little that was saved was again lost, or fell prey to malefactors, the unfortunate barely escaping with their lives. The loss is valued at three millions of dollars. In an affliction so cruel and so general, the only thing that can diminish our grief, is that not a man perished. On the morning of the morrow, what a spectacle was to be seen: in the place of the flourishing city of the day before, nothing but rubbish and heaps of ruins, pale and trembling mothers, dragging their children along by the hand, their despair not even leaving them the strength to weep or groan, and persons of luxury, quality, and consideration, who had only a stupor and silence for their

· · · · · · · · · · ·

one expression. But, as in most extremities, Providence always reserves secret means to temper them, this time we found, in the goodness and sympathy of the governor, and the intendant, all the compassion and all the assistance that we could expect from generous hearts, to arrest our tears and provide for our wants. They turned themselves to succouring us with so much order and diligence, that we were immediately relieved. Their private charities knew no limits, and the treasury of H. M. was opened to send away for assistance.

In a physical sense, the fire was actually beneficial to New Orleans. The buildings that replaced the irregular, asymmetrical, poorly planned structures dating far back into the French era were of a more sophisticated and

DETAILS OF IRONWORK ON THE CABILDO,
CHARTRES STREET, JACKSON SQUARE

. . . .

gracious sort. The motifs and patterns of the architecture that rose from the ashes of the French city created a markedly different ambience; rebuilt New Orleans had a more elegant, enjoyable, and suitably European face.

The enclosed inner courtyard (64), that mainstay of the Mediterranean home, was introduced at this time. This innovation made great sense in the tropical climate of Louisiana, as did the long, floor-length, louvered casement windows and airy colonnades and arches of the Spanish architecture. The new buildings were almost all constructed of brick, which made them structurally superior to the cypress log-and-plank buildings of the French town and gave them the added advantage of greater resistance to natural disasters. The brick walls were normally covered over with plaster, and both decorative and functional ironwork (174–5) appeared for the first time in the gates and balconies and terraces adorning the Spanish structures. It might be said that New Orleans' heritage of real architectural quality began at this point.

The entire conception of what a house should be had changed as a result of the fire's devastation. There was an openness to the new architecture, a sense of space both in façade and reality that had been lacking in the former buildings. The relationship of the inner, contained world to the outside became a more open one. Many houses were now built around central courtyards, with every room opening to a spacious expanse of sky and sun, the air circulating freely throughout. A great number of buildings presently standing in the French Quarter owe their conceptual dues to the Spanish design of this period. The flat, terraced roofs that adorned the upper stories disappeared in the early nineteenth century, but the attempt to reduce the scale of architectural elements in the buildings in order to accentuate the feeling of spaciousness left a lasting impression on the architecture of the Vieux Carré.

New Orleans' regeneration owed much to the generosity and humanity of one of its foremost citizens, Don Andrés Almonaster y Roxas, the wealthiest man in Louisiana at that time. The Don, an Andalusian nobleman, had arrived in New Orleans at the start of the Spanish rule and was appointed notary public, a position that opened up' many excellent business opportunities. In sixteen years, he had amassed an enormous fortune. With his great wealth secure, he married, at age sixty-two, an exquisite Creole girl. A devoted lover of the city that had been so generous to him, he set out after the fire to rebuild the school, then proceeded to pay for the parish church. This building, which would later become the Basilica of St. Louis (2), was designed by Gilberto Guillemard and cost $50,000. The colony's government was hard-pressed to pay for the great amount of construction required, and the Don dug further into his own coffers to construct an improved hos-

. . . .

pital, a rectory for the Capuchins, and a chapel for the aged Ursuline Convent, which had miraculously escaped the fire by virtue of the wall and garden surrounding it. (Ironically, the Capuchins, who had adamantly refused to sound their bells in alarm on Good Friday when the fire broke out, lost their monastery in the conflagration.)

The Don also paid for and initiated the construction of the most important governmental edifice to grace New Orleans, the Cabildo (*19*), the meeting place for the colony's administration. This imposing structure was erected at the north end of the Place d'Armes just to the west of the Basilica and replaced an earlier administration building that burned in another fire. The second Cabildo was a duplicate of the Presbytère (also ordered and paid for

· · · · · · · · · · · · ·

by Almonaster), which was located just to the east of the Basilica, thus combining the guiding institutions of state and church in an imposing one-block stretch. The Cabildo structure was completed in 1799, after the death of the Don, but it has remained a fitting monument to his public spirit. Today this old building still stands, impeccably restored to its original grandeur by Samuel Wilson, Jr., one of New Orleans' outstanding architectural historians and architects.

For nearly the first century of its existence, the destiny of New Orleans had been directed by forces distant from Louisiana. The grand gestures and secret dealings of European governments had been so consistently treacherous that the colonists were repeatedly forced to adjust to dramatic alterations in their lives, their homes, and their city. In fact, transformation and change had become the norm; the citizens understood that resistance would lead only to more suffering.

As the nineteenth century dawned, New Orleans lay on the verge of still another major change. The Spanish era of domination was grinding to a halt, and when the regime officially ended, on October 1, 1800, a sigh of relief went up from many of the Creoles who looked upon the return of New Orleans to the protective wings of Mother France as a blessing. As often happened, these expectations were to be short-lived. France dallied with the colony for the next three years, hesitating to accept responsibility for either its government or its welfare. While the city floundered in this neutral limbo, the sale of the Louisiana Territory to the United States for $15,000,000 had already taken place in Paris.

The possibility of a merger with the newfound republic was both un-attractive and preposterous to the Creoles. New Orleans was a hybrid Euro-pean city that combined a French and Spanish heritage, having no real ties to the American civilization that had evolved in the Northeast. The American "invasion" that followed met with resistance from the citizens of New Orleans. Their reactions were not subtle and they openly expressed their hostility toward the arriving "foreigners."

It is hard to imagine more different people than the Creoles and their new neighbors. The Latin population of the city was cultivated and sophisti-cated and had already earned a name and reputation for the special way of life it had developed in New Orleans. The institutions of Europe's refined culture were the best-loved traditions of New Orleans: the ball, the opera, the theater had advanced to a degree where they set the cultural tempo of the city. The often raw and coarse Americans grated on Creole sensibilities, and the Creoles had a difficult time enduring the invasion from "Kanetucky." The city had experienced few redeeming examples of American visitors be-fore the Louisiana Purchase, and for all they knew, the entire population of the United States were duplicates of the riverboatmen who could be counted on to tear up the waterfront whenever they arrived in town.

But there was no way to avoid the flow of Americans that continued to increase after the colony was delivered into the hands of General James Wilkinson and William C. C. Claiborne, Governor of the Mississippi Ter-ritory, on December 30, 1803. The official language of the land had been changed once again, this time to English, although the Creoles tried their best to ignore this edict. The snubbed Americans were forced to form a miniature society of their own. Since they were unwelcome in the Vieux Carré, they were compelled to search outside the existing limits of the city for homesites and succeeded in purchasing small plots to the west of the French Quarter on the farmland of the neighboring plantations. This new location, known as Fauberg St. Mary, would develop into New Orleans' first suburb.

When the city was passed over to America, the Ursuline Sisters feared that their property and convent would be confiscated by the new government, which was predominantly Protestant. Though the departed French and Spanish regimes had often been low on spirituality, at least they were Catholic through and through. The distraught Mother Superior wrote personally to President Jefferson to find out how he planned to act in regard to the Church. She received a letter in his own hand explaining that the division of Church and State provided for in the Constitution was to be maintained in New Orleans now that it was part of America. Indeed, New Orleans has remained a bastion of religious freedom and tolerance, enjoying a great reputation in that realm.

America west of the Alleghenies was experiencing a dramatic influx of settlers. As the land was cleared and towns sprang up along the major waterways of the Midwest and the South, the vast area began to develop rapidly. Of course, with the new markets and new produce created by the enormous growth came the problem of getting things to market. There was no practical way to bring large quantities of goods over the mountains to the marketplaces of the Eastern Seaboard, and the rivers of the region soon served as highways for transporting these valuables. New Orleans became the point of destination, whether the goods were bound for the East or abroad.

The South was simultaneously undergoing a dramatic swell in its production, as record profits began to flow from the cotton trade, and the huge plantations of sugar cane and indigo increased their output. Between the time of the Purchase and 1820, the volume of commerce increased enormously. With the invention and introduction of steamboats, the economic destiny of the city took its most significant swing upward.

It is safe to say that the steamboat did for New Orleans what the cotton gin did for the plantations of the South. This new and popular mode of river transport rapidly pushed the flatboats and keelboats off the Mississippi. The time involved in moving goods on the waterways was cut again and again, until in a few short years after the introduction of steam the river was covered with huge vessels moving their cargoes at a speed previously unimaginable.

. . . .

Almost overnight, river traffic doubled, then tripled, and in a short while New Orleans rivaled New York City for the distinction of America's busiest port. This enormous boom in transportation and trade marked the beginning of what is commonly referred to in New Orleans as its Golden Age.

Extending roughly from the Battle of New Orleans in 1815 to the advent of the War Between the States, this period was the era of the city's most rapid growth in every realm: economic, cultural, architectural, and aesthetic. The revenues that fell into the pockets of businessmen and traders who made and lost huge fortunes overnight while speculating on some commodity were of a dimension that put the city in an extremely desirable economic position. There was, for a time, no other place in America where such a concentration of wealth existed, or where it could be acquired as rapidly.

The boom of the eighteen-twenties and thirties in New Orleans was directly responsible for the physical expansion of the city in all directions, on a grander, more lavish scale than had been seen in any urban center of the South. The unique customs and culture, the heady climate and ever-improving materials combined to produce a definitive style of architecture and opened the way to that distinctively indigenous building that came to typify the great city.

. . . .

Shortly after the Americans began to build in the Fauberg St. Mary, people started to buy off lots in the old Marigny plantation to the east of the Vieux Carré, and by 1810 the Creole population was settling in the area that had been the plantation of Claude Trémé north of New Orleans' ramparts. The invading Americans had brought with them their own New England style of architecture, and American features began to appear in buildings that went up in the faubergs, and even in the Vieux Carré. The Georgian tradition, with its fanlight transoms (*153*) and balanced geometric proportions, is obvious to this day in such important buildings of the old city as the Hermann-Grima House.

Far from merely imitating New England style, Federal architecture evolved in New Orleans in its own special way, using local materials and adapting to local conditions. It also brought to the city's building a greater simplicity of façade and introduced curvilinear design and delicate detail. This mode is beautifully illustrated by the only extant work of America's first professional architect, Benjamin H. Latrobe, in his Louisiana State Bank (*103*) at the northeast corner of Royal and Conti Streets.

NEW ORLEANS SUGAR EXCHANGE

Credit: *Mugnier*

Many of the French architects of New Orleans became champions of Federal architecture. Among them were Hyacinth Laclotte, Jacques Tanesse, and Arsène Lacarrière Latour, though their designs always retained a tinge of their French Creole heritage. And as the century progressed, more and more Northern architects and builders moved to the Crescent City, bringing with them the immensely influential builders' and architects' handbooks by Benjamin and Lefever. Many interiors of this period, with their decorative plasterwork, mantels, dormers, and windows and doors, show the influence of these guides.

New Orleans had become the undisputed Queen of the Southern United States, rising to the position of its unofficial capital city. The flags of every great world power and republic flew from ships in the city's harbor awaiting the transfer of cargo from the riverboats, at the same time dispensing the finest goods that the world had to offer to the newly rich of the Crescent City, who were drawing on enormous accounts in the banks that lined Toulouse Street. Rare and precious materials, products and produce of every description were eagerly sought after, and what New Orleans didn't produce herself, she procured from her bulging lifeline to the world beyond the Delta. Even the ballast stones that filled the bottoms of the holds of merchant vessels were bought up by the city, which had, by the eighteen-twenties, finally become concerned with paving some of its streets. (These ballast stones can still be seen along the edges of streets of the Vieux Carré near the waterfront.)

When steam vessels appeared on the Mississippi, it was assumed that they would never be suitable for transporting passengers. The risk of human beings embarking on what were at first nicknamed "swimming volcanoes" seemed too great, but the American fascination for anything really new and unusual was an early national character trait. The boats became a popular and expedient form of human transportation almost overnight. This led to larger boats, designed to take cotton to market while their well-appointed cabins and extravagant galleries and parlors were filled with passengers. They were the first of the floating palaces, and before long the city's levee was choked with these great vessels docked three-deep into the Mississippi, their soaring stacks massed tightly in a dark cluster above the shaded decks. With the popularity of the riverboats, it became possible—even easy—for the curious and adventurous American citizen to hop aboard a river palace, and in unequaled splendor descend the muddy currents to the famous Delta boomtown.

Upon arriving in New Orleans, had he not been fleeced by one of the

countless cardsharps and professional gamblers who plied their trade on the great ships, this gentleman might make his way through the frenzied circus of the levee, overflowing with cotton bales, hogsheads, and roistering black stevedores, through the formal French garden in the newly renamed Jackson Square, past the handsome equestrian statue of the General himself, down Chartres Street, and up the steps into the sumptuous rotunda of the St. Louis Hotel. After refreshing himself in his suite and donning suitable attire, if the visitor was well connected he might meet with Creole friends, who would take him to one of the coffeehouses and cafés that lined Royal Street, to enjoy some absinthe. Then, his body bathed in the warmth of that mysterious liqueur, he might be treated to one of the most novel experiences the city could afford a visitor, the famed *bals de cordon bleu*, or quadroon balls.

Quadroons were the products of the union between a white man and a mulatto woman. If the mother had been a slave, she was probably freed by her lover so that their offspring would also be born free. As a quadroon girl grew up, her mother attempted to instill in her goals similar to those Creole mothers tried to implant in their daughters: namely, to set her aim on a well-to-do white gentleman who would provide her with the luxuries of life.

In the days of New Orleans' Golden Age, no custom proved more re-

. . . .

markable to an outsider than the institution of the quadroon balls. The sole intention of these gatherings was to allow the young white Creole males of New Orleans to select mistresses from among the quadroon girls attending these affairs. By this point in the city's history, the social structure and customs were very rigid and the quadroon balls were as much a part of the social traditions as the arranged marriages of the Creole aristocracy, where often the bride and groom never met one another until just before the nuptial ceremony.

The young quadroon women were raised by their mothers to fill a role similar to that of the geishas of nineteenth-century Japan. They were educated in as fine a manner as their Creole contemporaries and were steeped in the best aspects of life—verse, music, language, and art. They consequently enjoyed thoroughly cultivated backgrounds.

Descriptions from this era emphasize the exceptional beauty of the quadroons. They were the trend-setters of their day, and their distinctive flair and appearance set them apart from the rest of New Orleans womanhood. At a time when the typical woman's dress was dull and boring, the quadroons regularly appeared in public draped in the finest, most colorful silks, in designs that kept pace with the fashionable trends of Europe. Their style set them apart wherever they appeared and provoked a good deal of jealousy among the Creole ladies of the city.

With their exquisite beauty and cultivated accomplishments, the quadroon virgins were selected by their future consorts at the gala affairs held at the New Orleans Ballroom on Royal Street. Once arrangements had been agreed upon between the mothers (who were always in attendance) and the suitors, the quadroons were ensconced in small fashionable homes frequently located near the northern ramparts of the city along what was to become Rampart Street. Here they continued to be maintained by their lovers for what might be anywhere from one year to (in rare cases) a lifetime. Usually, the affair ended when the man got married, though many a married gentleman continued to make the pleasant jaunt to the rows of dainty cottages north of the Vieux Carré. If the arrangement was terminated by the Creole's wedding, the quadroon, as a settlement, would be allowed to keep the house and furnishings as her own property, and usually never embarked on another liaison as consequential.

Admission to the Orleans Ballroom at 717 Orleans Street was strictly restricted to white males, and although legends describing the ribaldry of these events spread far beyond New Orleans, they were without substance. In fact, the balls were decorous affairs that did not compare to the bacchanalian goings-on of the masked balls of the Mardi Gras.

. . . .

As American influence in New Orleans grew, the popularity of the quadroon balls decreased proportionately, and by the eighteen-fifties they were decidedly on the wane. When the War Between the States erupted and the quadroons found themselves alone and abandoned, with their consorts off fighting the Yankees, some of them married black men out of desperation, though these marriages were usually disastrous. After the war, they gradually vanished from New Orleans, either becoming assimilated into the black population or moving North.

The balls were often punctuated by another New Orleans tradition. Given the abundance of feminine pulchritude and the simmering passions of the young bloods, the slightest glance in the wrong direction or even some imaginary slight could easily lead to a glove being thrown and the inevitable *duelo*. The protagonists and their comrades would draw swords in back of the Basilica of St. Louis, where the sound of hard steel was heard as often as hoofbeats. At the height of its popularity, dueling was so common and frequent in the city that it was possible to find oneself in the position of having to accept a demand for "satisfaction" anywhere, anytime, and it seems, for almost any reason, no matter how innocent. The alternative was to leave the city and/or be ejected from the society of one's own peers. No social class or stratum of New Orleans's populace was exempt from this vengeful custom; even the brother-in-law of Governor Claiborne fell in a duel with a man who had criticized Claiborne's administration.

Like the quadroon balls and so many other traditions in New Orleans, dueling had been originally imported during the early days of the French in Louisiana, but in the Golden Age the popularity of the custom was carried beyond a reasonable frequency. In their own way, the laws in New Orleans managed to encourage dueling. There was a stiff penalty for anyone caught brawling or fist-fighting, and although dueling was officially frowned upon, there was no law against it on the books.

With these bloody encounters an everyday occurrence, fencing academies soon sprang up by the dozens, most of them located on Exchange Alley. These small enterprises were run by colorful fencing masters, many of whom became deservedly famous.

Among the more prestigious was Bastille Croquère, a mulatto reputed to be the handsomest man in the city, who pushed his sartorial display to the limit. Croquere was a stunning figure draped in his suits and capes of green broadcloth dripping with a splendid collection of cameos. He frequently met his opponents in this getup, which, however, in no way slowed his hand. His salon on the corner of Conti Street and Exchange Alley was usually filled to bursting with eager novices. Young Creoles returning from their studies in

Paris, as was the custom, would often round out their education under the tutelage of the mulatto master.*

Gilbert Rosière was another outstanding teacher whose fame in New Orleans was widespread during the Golden Age. In his prime, he was said to have fought seven duels a week. A complex man, Rosière was also very sensitive and gentle and was often seen weeping at the theater or opera during a poignant moment in the performance. Just such a display led to one of his most famous duels; a man seated near Rosière started to laugh at his tears during a tender aria and the master hastily challenged him. The two met the next morning at dawn under the popular "dueling oaks" in City Park, then a plantation outside the city. Rosière speedily overcame his opponent, but left him with only an ugly scar on his cheek as a reminder never to mock another man's feelings.†

If the visitor got safely through his evening at the quadroon ball and any ensuing duels, he might spend the next night at the theater. With its abundant wealth, New Orleans could afford to pay for and attract the greatest artists, actors, and singers of the day, and it supported a flourishing theatrical scene rivaled only by that of New York City.

Professional theater first arrived in New Orleans by way of a troupe of refugee French thespians fleeing the slave revolt in Santo Domingo. Under the direction of a Monsieur Tabry, they erected tents in a vacant square of the city and were soon playing to the applause of the enthusiastic Creoles. Shortly thereafter, the Santo Domingo troupe set up in a permanent location at 732 St. Peter Street. Known as Le Spectacle de la Rue St.-Pierre, this was the city's first real theater. Not only the élite of the great city flocked to the ticket window of Le Spectacle, but all levels of citizenry enjoyed the dramas and farces produced by these actors. New Orleans had come a long way from the days of *The Indian Father*.

In 1808, the St. Philippe Theatre (*33*), a classical and distinguished building, was erected on St. Philip Street between Royal and Bourbon at a cost of $100,000. The St. Philippe was the first theater in New Orleans to employ levels of tiers in its seating plan, and it held seven hundred people For the next twenty years it presented only the highest-quality dramatic fare.

By 1809, the even more opulent Orleans Theatre (*33*), designed by Lacarrière Latour, had opened. It served the public an excellent variety of theatrical presentations until it burned in 1813. Indeed, fire proved to be the chief enemy of New Orleans' theaters throughout the nineteenth century, and

---

* Saxon, *Fabulous New Orleans*, p. 192.
† Ibid., p. 194.

From Tanesse Map

almost every significant showcase sooner or later went up in flames. The Orleans Theatre was rebuilt in the same year by impresario John Davis, and the new building—still more elegant—included two rows of separate boxes, a gallery, and several dining rooms and bars. The exterior façade was embellished with Doric columns, and the balustrade around the roof supported a number of life-sized statues of romantic figures. In 1817, a ballroom costing $60,000 was added to the adjoining theater and gained fame as the traditional setting for the *bals de cordon bleu.*

Performances would usually commence at six in the evening and would continue well into the following morning. The entertainment might include an opera followed by a quadrille, then a light comedy or farce, and finally a serious drama or tragedy. This was the sort of bill presented for the Marquis de Lafayette when he spent an evening at the Orleans Theatre in 1825, viewing a performance held especially in his honor.

The theater world of New Orleans had originally been the exclusive domain of European actors, who were expected to perform in French. The costumes and sets for operas were also imported from France, a costly and inconvenient operation. In December of 1817, the first English-speaking drama was acted in New Orleans. This event was received so enthusiastically by the somewhat neglected Americans that by the next year two companies giving plays in English appeared at the Orleans Theatre.

. . . .

One of these troupes was under the direction of the actor James Caldwell, who was quick to notice the popularity of this form. He resolved to establish a permanent institution that would cater exclusively to English-spoken drama, and his enterprise led to the creation of the first St. Charles Theatre, unsurpassed in the grandeur of its design and appointment. The St. Charles was the first public building in town to be lit by gas. Caldwell had journeyed to Europe with the express intention of studying the Continent's most perfect halls and theaters in order to achieve the finest result in New Orleans. Once completed, the spacious hall seated 4,100 and was decorated with a gargantuan central chandelier 12 feet high and 36 feet in circumference, weighing 2 tons, with 250 gas jets lending their light to 23,000 glistening cut-crystal droplets, all suspended from the concave center of a heroic dome. However, the grandeur of the St. Charles was short-lived, since only seven years later the great building burned to the ground before the primitive engine companies of the city could put out the fire. On the same site, two of Caldwell's rivals, Sol Smith and Noah Ludlow, erected a second, less ostentatious hall, which stood until 1899, when in its turn it also caught fire.

With visitors such as our gentleman descending in waves as the commercial fortunes of the Golden Age blossomed, New Orleans was pressed to accommodate them in a manner worthy of her standing as the grand city of the South. The relatively small hotels that had served adequately before the eighteen-thirties were incapable of meeting the demands of the city's growth. To alleviate this problem, the Creoles set out to create a vast and luxurious institution that would serve a variety of social and community functions while housing large numbers of guests in a style commensurate with the times. The result was the Exchange Hotel, often referred to as the St. Louis Hotel. This impressive hostelry was designed by J. N. B. de Pouilly, a French architect. Completed in 1840, the hotel had a magnificent rotunda with an immense dome capping it. The rotunda of the St. Louis was frequently the sight of extravagant balls and was used periodically as a slave market where blacks were auctioned off from a block in the center of the palatial space.

In 1842 the Americans, not to be outdone by the Creoles, erected the St. Charles Exchange Hotel, designed by the firm of Dakin & Gallier. This was a vaster, finer building than the St. Louis and cost nearly a million dollars. The St. Charles was noted for its huge barroom, and the domed cupola that towered 185 feet above the street was the most famous landmark in the city, providing an unparalleled view of the Mississippi. The St. Charles was destroyed by fire in 1851 but was rebuilt soon after. The second version repeated Gallier's monolithic Greek façade of huge Corinthian columns rising to a classic pediment and heavy cornices. Unfortunately, this landmark, which dominated the American section of the city to the western side of Canal Street on St. Charles Avenue, was also the victim of a fire, in 1894, ending such splendid traditions as the famed golden service and menus serving over fifty entrées at a single meal.

While the great hotels and theaters were certainly the dominant presences in the architectural landscape of the city's environment during its heyday, the overall pattern of building and development had undergone drastic changes from the trends established in the eighteenth century by the original French and Spanish builders of the Vieux Carré.

At the time of the Louisiana Purchase, the Vieux Carré was already congested, and the squares of the Quarter left little room for further growth. The buildings were squeezed right to the edge of the banquette (the Creole term for sidewalk), with their sides flush against one another. Steady growth combined with hasty planning had resulted in this packed arrangement. The buildings lining the streets formed an unbroken wall that acted as a visual set for the public side of life, rigidly containing and separating the outer city from the inner, more peaceful sanctuary of the homes themselves. When a yard, a garden, or a patio adjoined a building, it, too, was inevitably walled off from the world outside. This sense of enclosure, of sealing off units spatially, occurs throughout the Quarter.

A typical Creole dwelling (59) sat flush against the banquette, concealing a court or garden in back. Behind this court was a service building (96), which, though separate, was usually tied by walls and court into the rest. The service building, in the rear or on the side, might be anywhere from one to four stories in height and had the appearance of a half-building; that is, a gabled structure sliced in two, forming a carpenter's-chisel roof (97). The front side of this outbuilding had a gallery with railings on its upper stories facing the enclosed courtyard. Like many of the houses, the service quarters were fashioned from the soft brick baked in one of the brickworks near town, then plastered over. The upper floors were the rooms of the slaves and servants of the resident family, while the ground floor contained the fires, hearths, and the kitchen, a feature that must have made the upper floors hellish in the severe temperatures of the summer months. The service quarters were sometimes larger than the main house, often containing storerooms, dining areas, and stables.

The courts were laid out in any number of shapes, depending on the piece of property and the proportions of the buildings. They were usually

. . . .

flagged or bricked, sometimes planted or containing a fountain, and one corner might hold a high, cylindrical cistern, which was used for collecting the water supply that ran off the roof of the service quarters.

The building techniques of the eighteenth-century Creoles continued to be used well into the nineteenth century. This is one of the reasons that much of the architecture of the Vieux Carré seems homogeneous. In addition, although the basic nature and design of residences eventually did change with the times, the trends that were in fashion at any given time were adhered to by most builders, architects, and homeowners, providing a great repetition of style and theme.

The Creole Townhouses (62, 63) of the Vieux Carré were substantial residences that might have anywhere from two to as many as four stories, with from two to four bays fronting on the street at each level. They were frequently built in speculative rows of from two houses to an entire block. The most common variety has three bays and is decorated with embellished lintels, transoms, doorframes, and moldings, varying in abundance or degree of refinement with the station in life and taste of the owner or builder. An interesting and popular variety is the Porte-Cochère Townhouse. This is a multistoried residence with a carriage passageway on the street level leading directly through the building and exiting in a courtyard, with stables in the rear.

A type of building found particularly on the corners is the Store House (83). These buildings were created to serve a multitude of purposes, for the lower stories served as businesses, shops, storehouses, or offices, while the floors above the street level contained the residences of the families engaged in commerce below. Many of these houses have fanlight transoms, which acted as sources of illumination just as the "eyebrow" windows (113) beneath the eaves ventilated the attics. This practical method of combining commerce with residence was a viable solution to the problems of city-dwelling in old New Orleans, allowing the entrepreneur to confine his cycle of activity to the space of a few floors.

The doors of both residences and store houses that fronted on the street frequently hung from iron straps and were usually solid, without openings. Occasionally the second story had a louvered gallery, and, as a rule, all the outer shutters of a house had louvers to help with the circulation of air. Dormers that acted as ventilators for the attics of buildings were another common feature. In the Vieux Carré, small dormers are ofttimes sided with overlapping squares of slate. These dormers appear on Creole Townhouses and Cottages, and also can be found in some of the later Greek Revival houses, a well-placed punctuation springing from the roofs of the buildings.

. . . .

A great many Federal-period façades in the Vieux Carré were altered significantly by the cast-iron work that came into vogue in the eighteen-forties. Often the ornamental iron lace first appeared as a replacement for decayed wooden railings, or when galleries or balconies were added to what had previously been unadorned fronts. These iron galleries changed the entire ambience and character of the buildings, as did the decorative iron brackets that supported the galleries from below.

During the Golden Age, the porch and gallery and balcony were the mainstays of the indigenous architecture of New Orleans and distinctly stamped the city with their look and pattern. They are a characteristic reflection of Creole sensuality and show a distinct attitude toward the world in their openness and presentation. With their outward thrust and overhang enfolding the light and air, they might be said to be the polar opposites of the courtyards. The citizens of New Orleans once loved to take the air from the height of a gallery railing ornamented with lush plant life and intricate iron arabesques. Above all, these were places for reflection and contemplation. There are still more porches and galleries in New Orleans than in any other city in America, and they remain a living artifact of over a hundred years' use.

The porch and gallery were innovations of the colonial French, modified and explored in the West Indian–style plantation houses that abounded in the environs of New Orleans. Prosperous planters built their manors on land-grant acreage handed out in the earliest days of settlement. These imposing residences often featured a steep hip roof with two or three dormers, a pronounced overhang supported by pillars that covered the front gallery, a rear gallery, and brick piers supporting the galleries, behind which were shuttered doors to the cool basements used for storage of perishables. This sort of manor-plantation house, with its full-length louvered shutters and doors on each floor, flourished in the Delta in the late eighteenth and early nineteenth centuries. They reposed, surrounded by cultivated fields, a world apart from the congested busy colony.

With the growth of New Orleans, the plantations, starting with those nearest the city, had been subdivided into plots that were gradually developed, plantation giving way to fauberg. It was this expansion into the faubergs, coupled with economic fortune, that resulted in the extravagant variety of architecture produced in New Orleans during the Golden Age.

At first, single houses here and there, along with a few plantation houses and outbuildings, were all that occupied the subdivided squares of the new faubergs. Following the Louisiana Purchase, the building rate increased significantly. Among the builders attracted to these semiurban areas were many freemen of color who erected homes of character, some of which still stand. However, they were far from the only people attracted by the relatively untouched expanses. The majority of immigrants arriving in New Orleans as the first half of the century progressed, the Germans, the Irish, the Italians, the Mexicans—and even Creole families—put roots down in the areas outside of what had been the original city.

Probably the earliest type of building in the faubergs was the Creole Cottage (*60*). Dating from 1810, it is the forebear of the myriad cottages and small houses that became popular as the century progressed. Cottages built in this period, like the houses in the Vieux Carré, were set right on the ground, with little attention given to a foundation, although after 1812 the design and methods of constructing the cottages gradually changed as a result of the American influence. The Creole Cottages originally were distinct in the steep pitch of their roofs, with eaves extending out over the street. The floors were flush with the banquette, and double doors and shutters were hinged on wrought-iron straps. The ancient method of split-timber construction with brick was used in constructing the tiny domiciles, and, as was the

1436 BOURBON STREET

custom, the brick and timber were usually plastered to seal out the elements. The cottages had gables on their sides and were straightforward, unadorned buildings. The greatest concession to decoration might be brick dentals forming a sawtooth row under the eaves. The eaves themselves were held up by iron supports that extended several feet out over the banquette, providing shade and protection from the rain and dampness.

The Americans instituted innovations in design in the cottages they erected throughout the faubergs, producing a type of building known as the American Cottage (*139*). These small houses were of a more classic and refined nature than the somewhat Spartan Creole Cottages. They borrowed heavily from the classical Greek Revival style that was sweeping the city by the eighteen-thirties, the era of the city's most phenomenal growth and expansion. They were set back from the street behind the typical white picket fences that lined the new subdivisions. In back of the fence would be a yard and often a garden, setting off the white pillared façade of the single-story cottage topped by its Greek pediment or Italianate cornice. The columns, as in all Greek Revival architecture, might take any number of shapes—boxed, fluted, or plain—pompous façades for diminutive houses.

The Greek Revival was by no means exclusive to the South, but in no other urban center was there the means or the necessity to produce this style in such abundance as in New Orleans. Consequently, despite the ravages of time, the city still contains the greatest assortment and variety of classic Greek Revival architecture in America. It is possible to walk for blocks and view nothing but almost uninterrupted expanses of classic Revival buildings with their forests of columns.

The sources of this form of design are entwined in the aesthetic and philosophy of those classic cultures that the adolescent United States idealized and admired in the early nineteenth century. The Golden Age of Greece was thought to represent the apex of Western civilization, and the infant democracy flourishing in America regarded this far-gone age as the time in history most worthy of emulation. It was not the first time that a civilization in the heat of new growth looked back in awe at the Greeks for spiritual inspiration, as the art of the Italian Renaissance testifies. But in the unique sociopolitical experiment of early-nineteenth-century America, it was the first time that the general populace could hope to live in a structure marked with such distinctive signs. Houses of this style expressed the viewpoint of the entire nation in its commitment to the restoration and application of the classic ideal.

The most lavish displays of Greek Revival in New Orleans rose on the green squares of the Garden District (*157*). The buildings were set far back from the street on generous plots, surrounded by trees and beautifully mani-

cured gardens. These houses were the true temples to American democracy, with their lofty colonnades, the etched-glass doors, the gleaming white façades, which almost reproduced the look of alabaster shining in the brilliance of the Southern sun. In the great houses, as well as in the small American Cottages and later the Shotgun Houses, the façade was usually accentuated, often with a raised parapet that created an effect of added height to the real weight and structure of the pediments and cornices.

The large grounds surrounding the houses in the Garden District and on such treelined boulevards as Esplanade Avenue succeeded in creating a sense of expansiveness that was in great contrast to the congested older portions of New Orleans. These parts of town emphasized a predilection toward the refinement of natural surroundings. Within the fences circling the property were formal French gardens drawn up in a style comparable with the most refined landscape architecture of Fontainebleau and Versailles. Walkways through arbors and hedges led to entryways beneath columned porticoes especially conceived to evoke the most auspicious air for passage into the interior. The doorways, with their beautifully carved casements and transoms, were masterpieces. Gates (*149*) were also an important feature of the formal entry plan, and when ironwork came into vogue, these lovely pieces of ornamentation were shipped in from as far as New York and Philadelphia.

The first Shotgun Houses in New Orleans were built in the Classic Revival eighteen-thirties, and were popular late into the nineteenth century. They were named for their interior layout, in which a number of single rooms proceed in sequence from front to back, theoretically enabling the resident to sit in the rear room of his house and, with all the doors open, fire a shotgun straight through the premises, to the dismay of bill collectors, traveling salesmen, and so forth. After the War Between the States, the gingerbread decoration characteristic of the Victorian period (*126*) often replaced the classic ornamentation.

Many ante-bellum Shotgun Houses have four-sided hip roofs, with chimneys at the central apex and service wings in their deep rear extensions. Fine examples of two-, three-, and four-bay Shotguns exist in almost every neighborhood of New Orleans. The size of these buildings is deceptive, because they extend very far back into their lots. They were an ideal way to economize on land, which was, by then, at a premium, for the long, deep Shotgun Houses could be packed very close together and still offer the buyer a number of rooms.

The Camelback (*117*), or Double Camelback, is a singular type of building indigenous to New Orleans, mainly because it doesn't seem to have caught on very well anywhere else. These curious houses have a single story,

usually featuring a low hip roof, which abruptly rises to a second story toward the rear of the building. The double version has two entryways and the interior is split in two to accommodate two families. These were by no means the only buildings divided in this manner; as far back as the Creole Cottages, houses were laid out to contain two separate living units. Some of the American Cottages and Townhouses were divided as well.

The eighteen-forties marked the appearance of the American Townhouse (*147*), which displayed a heavier, more imposing aspect than the earlier forms of Greek Revival. The crowning features of these houses—the cornices, pediments, and transoms—were of Italianate origin, and the builders did well in their imitation of cut stone or marble. The wooden sides of a building might be scored in a rectangular pattern to imitate masonry. There are instances where the entire façade was scored in this way, but most frequently it was done only at the corners of buildings to create the impression of cornerstones. The American Townhouses had even more elaborate entryways than previous styles, and the gable ends of both Greek Revival and American Townhouses were on the sides of the houses. The depth of the buildings varied with the property and the means of the builder, though most seem to have been fairly substantial and many even palatial.

By the eighteen-fifties, the city had spread and developed into an extensive metropolis that would probably have awed Bienville if he could have laid eyes on it. The scope and grandeur of the boulevards and upper-class areas, the mansions of St. Charles Avenue and the Garden District, the striking downtown American sector, and the treelined thoroughfares uptown and in the faubergs reflected the power and solidity of the great city. The dazzling whiteness of New Orleans, afloat on the bend in the river where the French colonists had first laid axe to the growth of cypress while clearing the land near Tchoutchouma, was a marvelous vision. Would Bienville have even recognized the Place d'Armes, with the handsome mansard roofs recently added to the Cabildo and Presbytère, and the block-long Upper and Lower Pontalba Buildings (45) stretching the length of the eastern and western sides of the square, their cherry-red bricks and voluptuous railings glistening and fresh?

These imposing structures were erected by the Baroness Micaela de Pontalba, daughter of Don Almonaster. Designed and built in 1849 and 1850, after the Baroness had returned to New Orleans from France, where she had lived since her marriage, the buildings are frequently referred to as the first apartment houses in America. Like so many stories relating to New Orleans, this is not true. Actually, the buildings each contained sixteen duplex townhouses with street-level storefronts. They were among the most fashionable residences in the city when they were built.

The outstanding ironwork, with the initials A-P for Almonaster and Pontalba, and the surrounding railings were designed by the Baroness herself. At first, the Baroness planned to retain James Gallier, the great architect of New Orleans' Golden Age, to design the massive buildings, but a dispute with him caused her to turn elsewhere, and both structures were the creation of the architect Henry Howard.

Unfortunately, most of the buildings Gallier did design no longer stand. This is one of New Orleans' real architectural tragedies, for by studying his exquisite drawings it is plain to see that he was the most creative designer of his age. Gallier, a native of Ireland, arrived in New Orleans from New York in 1834. He had learned his trade as a builder and later turned to architectural design. Once established, he rapidly became a champion of the classic Greek Revival style. His work was carried on by his son James, Jr. The interior of James Gallier's house on Royal Street (*following page 162*) reflects the manner and decoration of a well-to-do citizen of the Golden Age.

. . . .

It has been lovingly and authentically restored, and is one of the most elegant and charming interiors in the entire city.

Probably the most infamous house built in New Orleans during the Golden Age—a dubious distinction—is the mansion at 1140 Royal Street. Known popularly as "the haunted house," the massive gray structure provides a fitting setting for the legends of its strange and terrible past. The building was acquired by the daughter of the builder, Delphine LaLaurie, in 1831, and the beautiful Delphine and her husband entertained at gala banquets and gatherings beneath the sparkling chandeliers in the elegant interior of what was then the largest private house in the Vieux Carré. However, guests at their soirées could not help noticing that their glamorous hostess' servants

. . . .

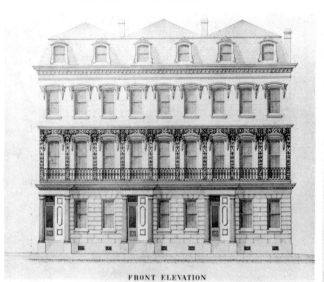

FRONT ELEVATION

— Elevation —

PLAN OF FRONT

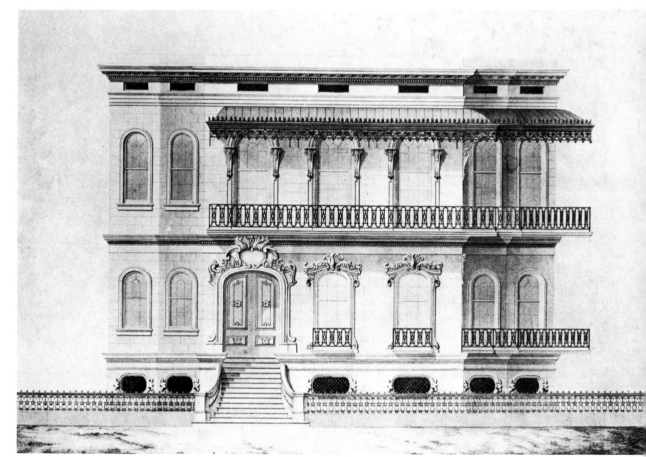

usually seemed subdued, emaciated, and slightly terrified as they went about their chores serving food and drink.

As was invariably the case in New Orleans, rumors started to spread about the peculiar demeanor of the LaLaurie servants, and this gossip was helped greatly by an incident witnessed by one of the neighbors. Hearing screams issuing from the mansion, the neighbor saw Madame LaLaurie chasing a young slave girl across the flagstones while brandishing a whip. The frantic girl rushed upstairs to the roof and hurled herself to her death in the courtyard below. Although Madame LaLaurie was taken to the station house following this incident, she was set free after being fined.

When a fire erupted on the night of April 10, 1834, neighbors broke into the mansion to rescue the priceless art objects from the flames. As the rescue workers burst through a door on one of the upper floors, they found some antiques of a different sort—whips, racks, and gruesome instruments of torture, along with seven LaLaurie slaves chained and pinioned to the walls in painful and grotesque positions. Once these macabre discoveries were made known, a mob massed outside the house, and as it prepared to take justice into its own hands, the black coach and horses of Madame LaLaurie burst through the gate and she escaped. The mob proceeded to loot the house in reprisal.

Although the house was restored after a short time, its occupants always seemed to be frightened off by strange noises in the night hours. No doubt, this is not the only "haunted house" in the city, but it is certainly the most well known.

As the fortunes of individuals shift and change, rise and fall, so with the fortunes of cities. Few residents of New Orleans—or the South, for that matter—were able to foresee the cataclysmic disasters wrought by the War Between the States that ended the Golden Age of the city forever. It could be argued that the growth of the railway would have eventually had the same effect on New Orleans' commerce, and it is true that by the eighteen-fifties its impact was already being felt along the levee and wharves of Decatur Street. But the changes brought by the iron horse cannot really be compared to the effects of the occupation that befell New Orleans during the war, an occupation presided over by the notorious General Benjamin "Silverspoon" Butler (so nicknamed because he sacked the Garden District of every piece of sterling his troops could get their hands on).

The raucous radical carpetbagging government that reigned over Louisiana during Reconstruction was not much better for the city. Consequently,

growth and building hardly resumed the proportions that had been common-place before the war, and the Victorian architecture which became popular during this period never reached the scale attained by the Greek Revival.

Many of the more striking Victorian structures in New Orleans are of the turreted Queen Anne variety (*190*), which was popular throughout the country during the late seventies and eighties. The whole concept of Victorian architecture, with its emphasis on the ornate, the extravagant, and the visual assault, had no problem finding acceptance in the wake of the futility and suffering that the city had experienced, and this style can be seen as a positive expression of new optimism. The overloaded and expressionistic design and ornamentation of the Victorian façades, with their capricious demeanor and almost comical overuse of adornment, created a lighter air, in pleasing contrast to the abundance of heavy, imposing buildings that had dominated New Orleans architecture for so long.

The mansard roof, introduced by architects who had brought it back from France, was only the first of hundreds of new shapes that were soon

Credit: Mugnier

HORTICULTURAL HALL, INDUSTRIAL COTTON CENTENNIAL EXPOSITION, 1884–85

Credit: Mugnier

· · · · · · · · · · ·

adorning the walls and porches of great and small homes. Stained and beveled glass began to find its way into the interiors of the more up-to-date residences, and the owners of many Garden District mansions at this time added to their Greek Revival houses exquisite beveled-glass doors (*following page 162*), with prismatic cut glass set into the leaded designs that covered the center portions of the doors.

With the industrial age picking up momentum in the second half of the nineteenth century, the utilization of standardized parts accelerated, and mechanized milling factories lent their technologies to the building trades. Every family in America had access to numerous catalogues that displayed brackets, moldings, railings, transoms, doorways, doorknobs, and virtually every part of a house or building—all for sale, all ready to order, delivered to a prospective builder through mail order. These catalogues had been used previously for ordering ironwork, and now that gingerbread was in style, they served the growing demand to embellish porches and gables with wooden arabesques and plaster pastrywork.

Shotgun Houses seem to have been the indigenous style that adapted most readily to the decorative Victorian mode. Countless small houses throughout the city went up with façades sporting extravagant jigsaw work on the gables, columns, spandrels, and porches and railings. The complex intricate embellishments of the Victorians made the cottages designed at this time (*118*) among the most charming works of this or any period.

New Orleans also built its share of ostentatious, baroque Victorian mansions—substantial Italianate, Gothic Revival (*191*), and Egyptian Revival homes—along with the more common stick-style houses, the mainstay of the era. Downtown, numerous Victorian office and commercial buildings (*88, 89*) rose along Canal Street and throughout the American sector. A number of these commercial buildings are still standing, although at present most are in danger of being torn down.

Probably the unique representatives of this most fantastic period of design, which seems to have emphasized the outrageous, are the Doullut Houses that sit on the edge of the Mississippi near the Orleans Parish line southeast of the Creole faubergs. These carbon-copy structures (*196*) were the work of Captain Paul Doullut, who took great pains to re-create the feeling of the numerous riverboats he had captained when he built them in 1905. The sentimental old river captain included such features as cupolas in the form of pilothouses, double metal smokestacks instead of brick chimneys, and railings, posts, and galleries reminiscent of the great Mississippi River queens that had almost vanished from the river when the houses went up. The buildings even include windows in the form of portholes. Fortunately, they have been well preserved and still remain in the hands of the captain's descendants.

The nineteenth century and the Victorian period drew to a close simultaneously as the country and the whole Western world moved into a more serious, less carefree time, and the curious and fanciful architectural creations of the Victorians soon gave way to an entirely different breed of design. What remained in New Orleans at the end of this period stands today as the most interesting collection of nineteenth-century urban residential architecture still in existence on these shores. From the forged-iron railings of the Creole Townhouses to the Greek Revival masterpieces that line Prytania Street to the high Victorian mansions of Audubon Place, the city's buildings collectively exude the special, rare atmosphere of the vanished Southern life style. And the epic of New Orleans' sensuality, passion, and fine living, combined with the widest expression and experience of life, is preserved for posterity in the city's buildings and houses. It is fitting that such an individual community, with its peculiar history and living traditions, remains for the most part intact and preserved, a monument to itself and its builders.

Here, for a time, life's greatest possibilities and adventures were realized and lived in the great houses of the French Quarter, the Garden District, the Uptown area, and the Creole faubergs. The Fathers of New Orleans built with a consistency that reflected their ideals and dreams, always keeping them foremost in mind as they created the tradition of sumptuous style which remains a tribute to that lost outlook and tempo, so foreign to the crazed pace of the contemporary world. This is the most important lesson of the great city, a lesson that will be understood and appreciated as long as her legends and buildings survive.

Afterword

. . . .

As America hurtles faster and faster into the last quarter of the twentieth century, changes continue to descend upon the nation with a rapidity that can only become more drastic, sudden, and irreversible. The magnitude of the shifts in the weight of our society and culture will wipe out more than a few aspects of our country that are of vast significance if we are to retain a sense of our roots and our heritage.

The people who live in the unusual, otherworldly city that is the subject of this book are in a position to hold on to one of the rarest, most interesting architectural environments in the land. There is not a single major urban center in the country that has met this challenge as well as it could have. The finality of the wrecking ball does more than destroy a building or a block; it cuts away the blood and vital cells that are a living part of the urban organism. Without the physical presence of an environment that has taken centuries to create, what else of value can people actually hope to hold on to? Memories and photographs are no substitutes for the living, breathing structure.

Fortunately for New Orleans, a great deal of its nineteenth-century body is still intact, and there are many individuals and excellent groups, such as the Friends of the Cabildo, the Garden District Association, and the Vieux Carré Commission, who are striving to preserve what is worth keeping in New Orleans' architectural landscape. It is up to the government and the individuals and the institutions of the city to take the initiative in joining those with like ideals to preserve and revere and protect their environment, which has, for most of this century, been taken largely for granted. The imagination and foresight necessary to carry this pressing task to its just, beneficial conclusion is a challenge worthy of the great city.

The Great Houses

. . . .

. . . .

BOARD OF TRADE BUILDING, BOARD OF TRADE PLAZA
(formerly the New Orleans Coffee Mart)

Indexes

. . . .

The figures in parentheses are house numbers; page numbers in italics refer to illustrations.

. . . .

. . . .